Paul Cézanne

*He saw the world
in spectacular shapes*

Written by
Amy Guglielmo

Illustrated by
Laura Martín

Paul Cézanne was born on January 19, 1839, in Aix-en-Provence, France.

His father, Louis-Auguste Cézanne, was the owner of a successful hat shop. The store did so well that Louis-Auguste had enough money to co-found a bank.

Paul had two younger sisters, Marie and Rose. Paul was only two years older than Marie, and so they attended elementary school together.

But Paul was closest with his mother, Élisabeth. He shared his dreams with her, and she encouraged his early drawings.

When he was 13 years old, Paul started attending the Collège Bourbon in Aix. There, he met his best friend, Émile Zola. One day, Émile would become a famous writer. Paul was a prize-winning student. He received awards for his skills in languages and math. His friends believed that he would become a great poet or writer someday!

Paul and Émile enjoyed going on adventures around the countryside of Provence. They both loved nature and hanging out on the banks of the River Arc. There, they fished, picnicked, swam, and spent time sketching, reading, and writing poems.

Go outside and sketch what you see.
Write a poem to go with your drawing.

In 1857, when he was 18 years old, Paul began attending the Free Municipal School of Drawing in Aix. He started thinking about becoming an artist even though he wasn't sure he was talented enough.

When Paul graduated from high school, he wanted to study art, but his father wasn't happy with this idea. Still, Louis-Auguste let Paul paint his portrait and several murals on the walls in the family home, *Jas de Bouffan* (The House of the Winds).

Louis-Auguste was a very strict man, and he encouraged Paul to study law or work in his bank instead. He didn't want his son to become an artist. To please his father, Paul attended law school in Aix for two years. But at school, Paul was miserable.

In 1860, when he was 21 years old, Paul decided he was done with law school, and he had to become an artist! With his mother's support, Paul convinced his father to let him go to Paris to follow his dreams. At last, his father agreed and gave him his blessing and a small allowance.

Paul's goal was to attend the École des Beaux-Arts in Paris, but first he had to be accepted...

Paul moved to Paris in 1861 and spent many days copying masterpieces by great artists at the Louvre Museum. Unlike the other artists, Paul didn't have to rely on selling his paintings to make money, because his father gave him an allowance.

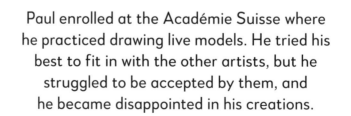

Paul enrolled at the Académie Suisse where he practiced drawing live models. He tried his best to fit in with the other artists, but he struggled to be accepted by them, and he became disappointed in his creations.

Find some scrap paper and draw some doodles.

Fed up, Paul returned to Aix after five months. He gave up his ambition of becoming an artist and went to work in his father's bank. When he was bored at his job, Paul doodled on bank documents. He spent all his free time drawing, and he started taking art classes again.

In November of 1862, Paul returned to Paris. This time, he was determined to make it work.

Artists in Paris at that time were painting portraits of nobility as well as smooth, fine scenes of historical events and mythology.

Paul made mythology studies and his own versions of the paintings at the Louvre, the same way the other artists practiced and learned. He worked hard to be accepted into the famous Salon: the official art exhibition of the Académie des Beaux-Arts. But when Paul applied to the Salon, where the most talented students from around the world studied, he was rejected.

At first, the painters Paul met in Paris thought he was strange and rude. Really, Paul was just irritated because he couldn't get his paintings exactly right. He used his canvases to express his feelings.

Soon, Paul started using darker colors and developed his own style of painting. He made loose, expressive brushstrokes and layered thick coats of paint on the canvas with a knife. Paul liked to paint ordinary people and everyday objects that made his work stand out when he applied to the Salon.

"I cannot convey my sensation immediately; so, I put color on again, and I keep putting it on as best I can."

Paul Cézanne

But Paul's art did not stand out in a good way. Once again, he was rejected by the Salon. He kept applying, but each time, Paul's paintings were dismissed. Frustrated, Paul would poke holes in his paintings, break his brushes, and throw some of his canvases into his fireplace!

While in Paris, Paul was influenced by other painters, including Claude Monet, Pierre-Auguste Renoir, Edgar Degas, Mary Cassatt, Berthe Morisot, and Paul's mentor and friend, Camille Pissarro. Some of these artists had also been rejected by the Académie.

This group of painters would eventually be known as the Impressionists. They paid special attention to light and captured moments of time in their paintings. Like Paul, the Impressionists preferred painting ordinary people and places, and they used dabs and short brushstrokes to create a scene.

"All the pictures painted inside, in the studio, will never be as good as those done outside."

Paul Cézanne

Claude Monet encouraged Paul to paint outside, *en plein air*, rather than sitting in a studio, and Camille Pissarro suggested that he try using brighter colors.

For a while, the artists painted together, *en plein air*, capturing scenes from nature. But after years of rejection from judges, professors, and critics, Paul was done with Paris.

Paul no longer cared what anyone else thought of his work. He decided he would make art in his own way.

When war broke out in Paris in 1870, Paul returned to the south of France to avoid military service. He brought his future wife, Hortense, back with him.

Paul was inspired by landscapes in the countryside. He took his friends' advice and painted in nature and used lighter hues. Sometimes he painted along with Camille Pissarro, and sometimes he painted alone from dawn to dusk.

Paul wandered through lavender fields until he found the perfect view of flowers smiling in the sun. With the sweet scent of honeysuckle floating on the breeze, Paul painted. He applied thick, mossy greens upon rolling golden hills, like sticky frosting on a cake.

Critics said Paul's landscapes looked flat because he didn't paint like traditional artists who showed distance and space. Paul worked hard to put his emotions into his work. He carefully captured the shapes, geometry, and colors that he saw in the distance.

To Paul, every stroke mattered, and he filled the canvas with a patchwork of layers. Claude Monet and other Impressionists could paint a scene very quickly. Paul would return with the same canvas to the same grassy knoll for weeks. Some landscape paintings took him years to complete.

"One minute in the life of the world is going by. Paint it as it is!"

Paul Cézanne

The Impressionists grew tired of being rejected by the Salon, so they decided to host their own show! In 1874, Paul returned to Paris to present his art at the first Impressionist exhibition.

Opening night caused a stir, but sales were not good. Critics called Paul's paintings "ugly" and "raw," and people laughed at his work. Paul skipped the second Impressionist exhibition.

Paul showed 17 paintings at the third Impressionist exhibition in 1877, but critics still didn't understand his unusual technique.

> ## "A work of art which did not begin in emotion is not art."

Paul Cézanne

Paul grew restless and didn't feel his style connected with the Impressionists. He was more interested in exploring the structures of his subjects than the light and mood of the moment, so he parted ways with his friends.

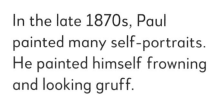

In the late 1870s, Paul painted many self-portraits. He painted himself frowning and looking gruff.

Make different expressions in a mirror to show emotions. Can you make a grumpy face? Now try a happy face.

Paul was struggling. In 1872, he and Hortense had a baby, but Paul still hadn't told his father about Hortense or his son. He wasn't selling enough paintings to support himself, and he feared his father would cut off his allowance.

Then, Paul met the art collector Victor Chocquet. Victor started collecting paintings by Paul, which greatly helped the artist financially. The two became good friends, and Paul asked Victor to pose for several portraits.

Paul famously worked very slowly. When he painted portraits, he often asked his subjects to sit very still for hours at a time. Paul had his art dealer, Ambroise Vollard, sit more than 100 times when painting his portrait! Sometimes the models fell asleep, and sometimes they grew bored and left. One of his favorite models was his future wife, Hortense. She patiently sat for more than two dozen portraits.

For many years, Paul painted throughout the French countryside, away from his family. Alone in Provence, he could work for long stretches of time without distractions. He would only stop to eat and sleep. When he returned home, he would retreat to his studio and paint some more.

The sun-drenched hills, luminous hues, and dramatic views in the region where Paul lived attracted and inspired other talented artists, too. While his friends worked beside him painting the changing light and colors of nature, Paul was dazzled by the solid shapes and geometric forms of the landscape.

In the south of France, he sometimes saw fellow artists Claude Monet, Paul Gauguin, and Pierre-Auguste Renoir. But mostly, Paul preferred to work alone.

Then, in 1882, one of his paintings was finally accepted for the Salon!

"Art is a harmony parallel with nature."

Paul Cézanne

Even though Paul's work was on display at the Salon in Paris, he continued to work in Aix. Around this time, Paul experimented with painting many different angles in a single piece.

In Gardanne, a village outside of Aix, Paul painted images of houses with diagonal lines and geometric structures. He used rich, bold patches of color and strong shapes to recreate the beauty of the scene.

"I paint, I work, I am free of thought."

Paul Cézanne

In April 1886, Hortense and Paul were finally married in the presence of his family. It had been more than 15 years since she first came to Provence!

Sadly, in October of that year, Paul's father died. Paul inherited enough money to support his family. The money also gave him the freedom to paint the way he pleased without having to worry about selling his art.

While other artists concentrated on landscapes, Paul became interested in still life compositions. He was constantly trying new things and playing with different ways of seeing and portraying objects.

Gather a few objects to make a still life arrangement.

Which objects did you choose?

In traditional still lifes, artists arranged fruit, flowers, and everyday objects, and painted them exactly as they saw them. When arranging and painting his still lifes, Paul fixed his attention on the shapes, forms, and colors of the objects and showed multiple views all at once: from above, straight on, and sideways.

Sometimes Paul spent so much time on each painting that the fruit would shrivel and spoil. Paul mostly avoided using cut flowers because they would wilt and die, so he used potted flowers instead.

The artist Claude Monet was an enthusiastic gardener. He bought Paul's painting *Still Life with Apples and a Pot of Primroses*. Paul used thick paint, layered colors, and directional lines to show the solid forms of the objects.

"With an apple I want to astonish Paris."

Paul Cézanne

His still life paintings of apples became some of his most famous artworks.

In the early 1890s, Paul became interested in painting the ordinary people around Aix. He painted the farmhands from his family estate playing cards at the local café. Just like in his still life paintings, in Paul's series of paintings *The Card Players*, he arranged the compositions and posed the models precisely.

Invite your *friends* and *family* to pose for a picture. Arrange them doing an activity like **playing** a game.

"He [Cézanne] can't put two strokes of color on a canvas without it already being very good."

Pierre-Auguste Renoir, artist

For many years, Paul worked alone in the countryside. The public rarely saw his finished pieces. Eventually, in 1895, Paul was given his first solo exhibition. He was 56 years old. Art dealer Ambroise Vollard hosted the show at his gallery in Paris. The paintings included Paul's majestic landscapes, his marvelous still lifes, and several portraits of Hortense.

Before the show, the people who collected Paul's work were mostly his friends and fellow artists. On opening night, the patrons were truly astonished! The exhibition was a huge success. Collectors and artists purchased many of the works on display.

At long last, some critics were charmed. They praised Paul's enthusiastic use of color and unconventional techniques. They called him a true revolutionary for overturning the traditional rules of painting.

Back in Aix, Paul retreated from the attention. He dreaded hearing the comments from critics, but he also hated hearing praise and couldn't take a compliment.

"My hair and beard are longer than my talent."

Paul Cézanne

When his mother died in 1897, Paul was heartbroken. He painted his grief instead of attending her funeral. For a while, Paul withdrew from his family and other artists unless he was painting their portraits.

In 1899, Ambroise Vollard bought all the paintings in Paul's studio. He needed more work because Paul's paintings kept selling, even after Ambroise raised the prices.

Throughout his career, Paul would return to pieces he'd started, adding new dots of color from time to time. As a result, many of his pieces remained unfinished or works in progress. He signed very few of his paintings, but his art dealer didn't mind. Ambroise took those paintings to Paris too, because he knew they would sell!

Paul's modern and abstract style of painting gained a following among artists who were just starting out in Paris. They appreciated his fresh approach and the freedom of expression they saw in his compositions.

By 1901, Paul's work had achieved fame across Europe. Aspiring young artists came to Provence to learn from him.

If you had the chance to meet the artist *Paul Cézanne*, what questions would you ask him?

During his later years, Paul's health got worse, and he painted mainly in Aix. There, he painted, revised, and repeated his favorite mountain scenes and his humble apple portraits. His work grew more abstract and even bolder as he continued to push boundaries in art.

Starting in the 1880s, Paul made a series of paintings of Mont Sainte-Victoire. He painted his beloved scenic mountain from different points of view and in all the colors of the rainbow.

Paul pledged to paint until the day he died. In October of 1906, he was painting outside on his favorite lookout when he was caught in a storm and collapsed. He fell ill with pneumonia and died just a few days later.

"...*I am old and sick, and I have sworn to die painting* ..."

Paul Cézanne

In 1907, an exhibition at the Salon d'Automne in Paris featured 56 of Paul's paintings. Everyone in the city was talking about his legacy. Paul's new and different style of work has influenced famous painters, including Paul Gauguin, Pablo Picasso, and Henri Matisse. Pablo Picasso called Paul "My one and only master... Cézanne was like the father of us all."

PAUL GAUGUIN

PABLO PICASSO

HENRI MATISSE

During his lifetime, few people besides other painters recognized Paul's role as an important and transformative artist who saw things in his own way. Today, Paul Cézanne is considered "the father of modern art." He is celebrated as one of the most popular artists in the world. His paintings are now considered masterpieces and hang in museums all around the world.

Timeline of key artworks

During his career, Paul Cézanne created many still life paintings, portraits, and landscapes using bold dabs of color and unconventional techniques. Here are a few of his key works of art that feature his spectacular style. All of them can be found in the collection of The Metropolitan Museum of Art.

No date
Portrait of the Artist (recto); Fragment of a Landscape Study (verso)
Graphite

1866
Antoine Dominique Sauveur Aubert (born 1817), the Artist's Uncle
Oil on canvas

1882–85
Mont Sainte-Victoire and the Viaduct of the Arc River Valley
Oil on canvas

1885–86
Gardanne
Oil on canvas

ca. 1890
Still Life with Apples and a
Pot of Primroses
Oil on canvas

"I am still striving to discover my right way as a painter. Nature puts the greatest obstacles in the way."

Paul Cézanne

1891
Madame Cézanne
(Hortense Fiquet, 1850–
1922) in the Conservatory
Oil on canvas

Timeline continued:

1890-92
The Card Players
Oil on canvas

ca. 1891-92
Still Life with Apples and Pears
Oil on canvas

1892-94
The House with the Cracked Walls
Oil on canvas

ca. 1892–96
Seated Peasant
Oil on canvas

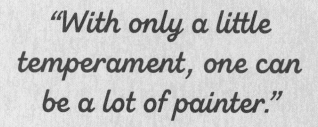

"With only a little temperament, one can be a lot of painter."

Paul Cézanne

1893–94
Still Life with a Ginger Jar and Eggplants
Oil on canvas

ca. 1902–6
Mont Sainte-Victoire
Oil on canvas

Landscape En Plein Air

Paul Cézanne was inspired by the scenery of the countryside near his home in the south of France. He painted landscapes to capture the colors and feelings he found in nature. Critics said Paul's landscapes looked flat, because he didn't paint like traditional artists who showed distance and space. Instead, he liked to capture the geometry and shapes he saw in nature.

ca. 1902-6
Mont Sainte-Victoire
Oil on canvas

Paul Cézanne painted many versions of Mont Sainte-Victoire near his hometown of Aix.

Now it's your turn!

Go outside and paint or draw *en plein air.*

Paul Cézanne expressed his emotions on his canvas. Try working in nature to capture your feelings in a work of art. Find a view or a scene that makes you feel something. Using paper and a pencil, sketch an outline to show what you see.

Try this yourself!

"To paint from nature is not to copy an object; it is to represent its sensation."

Paul Cézanne

Still Life Fruit Series

Paul Cézanne famously made still life paintings using fruit, like apples and pears, because they grew where he lived. Paul rarely made pictures of fresh flowers because he would paint so slowly, they would droop and wilt. Like his landscapes, Paul focused on the shapes, forms, and colors of the groupings. His still life paintings showed multiple views all at once: from above, straight on, and sideways. Now, you try!

Your turn!

ca. 1890
Still Life with Apples and a Pot of Primroses
Oil on canvas

During his life, Cézanne painted more than 100 still lifes. Gather some objects that are special to you. Arrange them on a table and draw or paint them.

Be like Cézanne!

"When you see a Cézanne, it's like seeing the moon — there's only one moon, there's only one Cézanne."

Max Weber, artist

Paul Cézanne liked to repeat, rework, and remake images using the same vases, objects, cloths, and backgrounds so he could learn from his own compositions. Using the same objects, rearrange the groupings and make a series of still lifes!

Stack books or boxes on a flat surface and cover them with a cloth to create a setup with different levels. Place your still life objects on your new setup and sketch the different shapes you see. How do objects look different from different angles? Color in your shapes using pencils, pens, paints, or colored crayons to add texture and details.

Glossary

Composition
The arrangement of elements in a painting or other work of art.

Copyist
An artist who makes drawings, paintings, or other works of art in the style of other artists to improve their skills.

Critic
A person who judges the merits of a work of art.

En plein air (in the open air)
A manner of painting outdoors that became a central feature of French Impressionism.

Geometric
The arrangement of lines to create shapes such as squares, triangles, or rectangles.

Impressionists

A group of artists in the late 19th and early 20th centuries who painted scenes of everyday life with lively brushstrokes and vivid color and paid special attention to the changing effects of light.

Landscape

Art that depicts the natural environment.

Modern art

Art created from approximately the 1860s through the 1970s. Modern artists reject traditional techniques of the past in the spirit of experimentation.

Portrait

A work of art created to show a person, animal, or group of people, usually focusing on the face.

Salon

An annual exhibition of the work of living artists held by the Académie des Beaux-Arts in Paris.

Still life

A painting or drawing of an arrangement of objects, such as flowers in a vase or fruit in a bowl.

Amy Guglielmo

Amy Guglielmo is an author, educator, artist, and community arts and STEAM advocate. She has written many books for children, including *Cézanne's Parrot* and *Just Being Dali: The Story of Artist Salvador Dali*. Amy has coauthored the picture books *Pocket Full of Colors: The Magical World of Mary Blair*, winner of the Christopher Award; *How to Build a Hug: Temple Grandin and Her Amazing Squeeze Machine*; and the *Touch the Art* series of novelty board books featuring famous works of art with tactile additions. She lives in New York and Mexico with her husband.

Laura Martín

Laura Martín is an Argentinian illustrator and graphic designer based in Berlin. She worked as a children's editorial designer and illustration assistant for almost a decade before becoming a full-time freelance illustrator. She's curious by nature and loves to research all kinds of topics. Her inspiration comes from very diverse sources: nostalgia, friendship, music, books, personal experiences, and simple and happy moments of life. When she's not drawing, you can find her listening to 80s music, playing the piano, traveling and exploring new places, drinking coffee with friends, or just spending time outdoors.

Project Editor Rosie Peet
Editor Vicky Armstrong
Project Art Editor Jon Hall
Art Director Clare Baggaley
Production Editor Siu Yin Chan
Senior Production Controller Louise Minihane
Senior Acquisitions Editor Katy Flint
Managing Art Editor Vicky Short
Publishing Director Mark Searle

First American Edition, 2024
Published in the United States by DK Publishing
1745 Broadway, 20th Floor, New York, NY 10019

A catalog record for this book
is available from the Library of Congress.
ISBN 978-0-7440-9223-3

DK books are available at special discounts when purchased
in bulk for sales promotions, premiums, fund-raising, or educational use.
For details, contact: DK Publishing Special Markets,
1745 Broadway, 20th Floor, New York, NY 10019
SpecialSales@dk.com

Printed and bound in China

Acknowledgments
DK would like to thank Josh Romm, Laura Corey, Amy Charleroy, and
Rachel High at The Metropolitan Museum of Art; Jennifer Moore for
fact-checking; and Meghan McCullough for proofreading.
The author would like to thank Mark and Kristi Giebel.

www.dk.com
www.metmuseum.org

Picture credits
The publisher would like to thank The Metropolitan Museum of Art for their
kind permission to reproduce works of art from their collection.

Antoine Dominique Sauveur Aubert (born 1817), the Artist's Uncle (1866). 53.140.1; *Portrait of the Artist (recto); Fragment of a
Landscape Study (verso)* (no date). 1972.118.198; *Mont Sainte-Victoire and the Viaduct of the Arc River Valley* (1882–85). 29.100.64;
Gardanne (1885–86). 57.181; *Still Life with Apples and a Pot of Primroses* (ca. 1890). 51.112.1; *Madame Cézanne (Hortense Fiquet, 1850–1922)
in the Conservatory* (1891). 61.101.2; *Still Life with Apples and Pears* (ca. 1891–92). 61.101.3; *The Card Players* (1890–92). 61.101.1;
The House with the Cracked Walls (1892–94). 1993.400.2; *Seated Peasant* (ca. 1892–96). 1997.60.2; *Still Life with a Ginger Jar
and Eggplants* (1893–94). 61.101.4; *Mont Sainte-Victoire* (ca. 1902–6). 1994.420